The (Forever) Beginner's Meditation Companion

(From the "Meditation for Non-Meditators" Series)

By
Tina Foster

Also Part of the Meditation
for Non-Meditators Book Series:

*Meditation for Non-Meditators: A (Forever) Beginner's
Guide,* a book of guided practices

Table of Contents

The (Forever) Beginner's Meditation Companion

Introduction

About this Companion

Take a moment to remember a close companion in your life—a friend, family member, lover, or pet.

You might see their face, hear their voice, or sense that special something that first drew you to them. Your heart might warm or feel bittersweet.

Now remember the quality of the companionship itself—that rare and one-of-a-kind fusion of You + Them. Your unique blend of personalities.

What do you cherish most about this companionship? How did it support you or change who you were? What did it show or teach you?

Quite likely, this friend also had their own special way of setting you straight, applying a bit of tough love, or calling you on your BS. Or maybe being around them was enough to automatically bring out your personal best.

I've come to see meditation as this kind of companion. It has the power to lift your mood, help you find courage, or just sit there with you when you need solace. It can take you on a wild internal joyride or the opposite—bring you back to focus on your routine or goals.

Here's another way meditation is like a living companion. There's a living relationship involved that requires effort and respect to maintain.

Compassion, humor, and honesty will foster healthy companionship.

And the opposite can be true. Meditation practice can become an obligatory relationship. It's the friend you dread meeting.You always seem to scrap with each other, but you just can't let go.

Meditation fosters responsibility and accountability. You tend to notice how you show up to the practice relationship, what you hold as you arrive, what you leave with, and what choices you make during the highs and lows.

So, the first piece of advice is to think of your meditation practice as a relationship that you cultivate, rather than a task you're trying to do well.

If you nurture your practice, it nurtures you in return (more about this in "Mindfulness mediums").

The companion's companion

This book is the companion I wish I'd had when first trying meditation.

Even in a group practice, I sat alone. I pretended to know what I was doing.

I joylessly followed the instructions of my teachers and felt like a fake. There's nothing necessarily wrong with the "fake it till you make it" approach in life—up to a point. But I often sat "in meditation" feeling pain, anxiety, and guilt, wondering what do about so many issues that weren't part of the guidance.

During actual meditation practice, as we sit, usually with eyes closed, we need more guidance than instruction.

What do we mean by guidance?

Guidance is more like having someone hold our hand or nudge us along as we make our way. Guidance inspires our curiosity rather than prescribing our thought processes.

Being guided isn't like being lead. Guided practice tends to allow long moments of quiet and freedom to poke around our inner terrain.

But even with the best guidance we can sometimes get lost during practice, which can be like stumbling through a noisy, foreign city with unmarked crossroads and only the vaguest idea of where to turn. ("Mindfulness mediums" also talks more about these crossroad moments and how to know which way to turn.)

This is where instruction comes in. Even a little instruction before practice helps us feel more confident and safe about finding our way around our inner terrain.

So, what defines instruction?

Instructions often contain guidance. Their job is to teach us and get us thinking about our process.

Instruction is more thorough than guidance and is more likely to employ a "no stone unturned" approach, covering as many topics as possible.

Instruction asks us to learn about practice from the outside, while guidance helps us navigate inside of our practice.

Finding our way is much more fun when we open up to meditation practice as an exploration rather than a test, but we need trustworthy instructions along the way.

This book provides comprehensive instruction about meditation as an overall practice and as a specific technique—as well as what its components are and how these components are used.

Approach meditation as your companion. Use this book as your companion's companion. Remember, embrace meditation and let it:

- Walk shoulder-to-shoulder with you along your journey
- Invite rather than obligate
- Take the lead when the way is unclear
- Challenge you and nudge you along

This book will continually point your compass towards home (that is, to yourself) because meditation is self-companionship. And self-companionship is the root of all the best friendships, right? Great friends are first friends to themselves.

I also wrote this book as a companion to the three guided meditations in my first book, *Meditation for Non-Meditators: A (Forever) Beginner's Guide*. However, this book promises to be a handy companion to any practice you undertake.

How to use this book

Imagine a companion that shows up before and after meditation time with a toolbox to help you build a practice that's designed for you, fix whatever you break, and continuously redesign as your practice grows.

Pretty soon, you'll be using these tools to do your own design and repair until you have a practice that's a safe, efficient, comfortable, and portable sanctuary that adapts to your evolving needs. (In "The inner toolbox," we look at various tools we can use to build the best practice possible, and how we can sustain and evolve it over time.)

Now, a bit about how this book is built.

Chapter breakdown:

Chapter 1:True Beginnings offers metaphors that help us understand what meditation is, what it's like to practice, and how and why to build meditation roadmaps.

"True Beginnings" will get the wheels of your imagination turning, fire up your curiosity, and inspire you to practice. You'll visualize theory and see how theory works through story and scenario.

In Chapter 2: Forever Beginnings, we open the meditation companion's toolbox, look at these handy practice tools, and think about what each one is good for.

We'll also examine the mediums through which practice can flow: Mind, body, emotions, the senses, and breath.

"Forever Beginnings" also sheds light on the nature of thoughts, their patterns, and how a computer hard drive is an evocative metaphor for the mind.

The metaphors and stories deepen our understanding of theory. We get to a point of understanding where theory is able to stand on its own, naked, so we can see it for what it really is.

Then, Chapter 3: The Glow and Flow of Insight sheds light on the moments when practice has become more natural, smooth, and free. We learn how to spot early signs of insight and growth as they occur during practice.

Next we'll look at Nirvana, which isn't necessarily the destination of practice, but is the most actualized—some would say idealized—experience of meditation.

So, "The Glow and Flow of Insight" is the chapter that reveals the ties that hold the meditation process together. We bundle up the stories and theories as one big, broad evolving process.

There's plenty of practicality in the first three chapters, but the final chapter (Chapter 4: Horizons Everywhere, Forever) is where the practicality moves from story and theory to utility. The final chapter is all about how to...., what to do when..., avoid this... and look for that.

It lists how to map out your overall journey from the outset, what to do before each session, and how to prepare for the odd or unusual things that can happen during practice (like falling asleep) as well as the peaceful and ecstatic moments (such as sudden Nirvana-like bursts of inner joy).

We'll also learn how meditation can be a companion in tough times, what to do when you don't have time to practice, and what happens when you drive yourself into a meditative ditch. (Spoiler alert: There is no true meditation-fail.)

The conclusion gets philosophical about choosing and building the practice that's right for you, and recognizing what works versus what doesn't.

Meditation is a practice of forever-beginning as well as a continual returning home. This book is an eternal companion that you return to again and again for practical help and a friendly nudge, whether you're practicing with the Meditation for Non-Meditators guide or another source.

There are infinite ways to move through these pages.

The simple, straightforward way: Non-stop, chronologically, cover-to-cover in about an hour.

Or the opposite: Dropping in as needed (each time scanning for a particular information nugget), zipping back to practice, nugget in hand, to drop the wisdom into your practice mix, and eventually reading every page at least once, yet never reading cover-to-cover. Two different ways through, two very different experiences.

Chapter 1

True Beginnings

Map out a plan

Your companion has a meditation roadmap. She shows you different ways to make your journey and allows you to choose your own route. You get to decide whether to take the easier or more challenging route. Do you play it safe with a tried-and-true path or risk the road less travelled for the sake of adventure and discovery?

Don't be tempted to blaze a trail without your compass pointing in the direction you intend to go. Decide where you want to go and how you want to get there. Take some time to plan.

Some people like to plan, some don't. But here's one undeniable thing about a plan. When you're lost with no idea where to turn, The Plan is there to fall back on, saving you from getting stymied or having to make rash decisions. ("The Nitty-gritty of meditation-mapping" will guide you through the practical steps needed to create an original roadmap for your unique practice. Even if you hop over there now to read them, definitely read them again later and consider taking the recommended actions before you begin a practice session.)

I want to touch briefly on one particular recommended action right now: The benefits of keeping a meditation journal. I didn't keep a meditation journal. I don't think anyone ever advised me to.

I learned of the benefits of meditation journaling in hindsight. From time to time, I'd stand up from practice and scramble to scribble down a thought, idea, feeling, sensation, or experience. Usually, I was hoping to capturea crystal clear realization, or the opposite—a puzzling experience I barely had words for.

I wrote on whatever was available, a napkin, a slip of paper, or even my arm. Sometimes I kept the napkins and slips of paper, but never for very long. And I never collected all the fragments into a single pile.

Writing things down was certainly better than nothing. However, had I recorded all those ideas and mysteries in one place, this book would have been written way, way earlier.And at this very moment of writing, I'd know far more about meditation than I currently do.

Keep a meditation journal.It's not vanity, narcissism, or self-indulgence. As you'll soon learn, a journal serves as a map made from a map. A re-map.

Re-mapping

The Plan you make using the considerations in the last chapter of this book will be your original map, the route you imagine taking before hitting the meditation road.

The record you keep in your journal becomes your second map, the real route as best you know it, compiled over many journeys and continual re-mappings.

Now imagine these maps drawn on transparencies. Superimposing one on top of another reveals a more complete and realistic picture of your journey.

Keep re-mapping.

What is meditation?

Let's get clear on what meditation is before we take off. The definitions of "meditation" in this companion book are threefold:

Meditation as practice. This is the act of meditation: What we do, the instructions we follow, and the techniques we use.

Examples of this definition: "How to practice meditation" and "How to meditate by listening to sound."

Meditation as experience. This is what happens as we practice—not what we do, but what we encounter and the reactions (or lack thereof) that the experiences trigger.

Examples of this definition: "What is meditation like?" or "Yesterday's meditation practice was like pulling teeth."

Meditation as process and purpose. This is a fusion of practice and experience: How we encounter (not just react to) our experience; How we navigate the big picture and respond momenttomoment; What strategy or direction we take to stay on track.

Examples of this definition: "The process of meditation is to re-focus each time I become distracted" or "Meditation practice shows us a way to relax while paying closer attention."

As we practice meditation over time, the instructions we follow begin to feel less contrived and more fluid. Our experience begins to inform our process. The more skillful our process, the closer we come to our purpose and the smoother we ride.

The purpose of meditation: Finding reality in empty spaces

The purpose of meditation is to get real, not check out from reality. This becomes apparent over time. Once we're less stressed and distracted, we're more likely to see reality through a cleaner lens.

The practice of meditation takes us beyond the noise of our daily lives. At first we find stillness and quiet, then eventually snips of a deeper reality inside the stillness and quiet.

Let's look closer at this idea.

What lies beyond (and even between) the thoughts, noises, and distractions are "empty spaces." Entering an empty space is like moving from a noisy room to a quiet one. The mind and body sigh with relief.

At first, we might not actually experience empty spaces for what they are. Either they aren't anywhere to be found, or we're unable to notice them amongst all the thoughts, noises, and distractions.

The very first empty spaces we experience often appear in flashes, coming and going in a nanosecond.

These momentary empty spaces are often compared to the spaces between the cars of a passing train. Each train car has its own shape and color. Some are old and rusty, some new and shiny.

Our attention is initially drawn to the cars rather than the blurred spaces between. Yet, something deeper about reality lies on the other side of the train, viewable only through the spaces between the cars. We move from thinking the cars are everything to seeing them as an obstruction to this deeper reality.

What's inside empty space?

For the sake of moving into an empty space, imagine you're the conductor of this train.

You're in the engine car looking ahead onto the tracks. The train rolls into a dense urban area. You see a clutter of buildings and roads. There's plenty of sound, movement, and beauty to capture your attention—like brilliant neon signs and people in fancy suits. There's a palpable feeling that anything can happen. As the conductor, you're trained to navigate through the distraction and stay on track.

This urban area is like the surface of our minds, a dense and dazzling wall of distraction blocking us from empty space. We move through this wall in layers. It might take years of practice to get through.

We still notice potential distractions as we make our way. In fact, the distractions might intensify as we get closer to empty space. We don't exhaust ourselves by fighting off distractions or desperately trying to claw through the wall.

As you conduct the train out of the city, the urban density fades into a huge open desert. Suddenly, there's no noise, buildings, or people. Not even a tree. There's nothing anywhere. Or is there? Past experience rolling through open desert has taught you otherwise.

You adjust to the more open, quieter landscape, but you don't daydream. Instead, your attention begins to perceive greater subtlety. You begin to notice things you'd otherwise miss—a deer hiding in the brush or a lone palm tree on the horizon.

You know plenty of things could go wrong in this landscape, but you're ready for any sudden changes. You stay aware because you still have to drive the train.

This desert is like the empty space in our consciousness where a more nuanced experience awaits us. As we anticipate this nuance to be revealed (especially if we've just been in a noisy space) we might feel impatient or even uncomfortable.

Naturally. In the noisy space, we were letting all the stimuli fall to the background.

Now, in the more open space, we're doing the opposite, waiting for information we can take in. Or so it seems. We may feel an urge to fill this emptiness with something. But we trust our process and keep going.

As we become familiar with empty space, the transition from noise to quiet becomes less awkward. Like the train conductor in the desert, we know that empty space really isn't empty at all.

Within the quiet of our deeper layers of consciousness is a world of boundless insight and creativity. The more we enter this subtler space in meditation, the more insight and creativity we uncover, and the more real we become in our own lives. (More on empty spaces and deeper consciousness in "Effortless insight.")

Standing on the shoulders of giants

Remember, meditation is universal and is thousands of years old. As a formal practice, it's been passed down for generations.

Each generation stands on the shoulders of giants—its teachers, guides, and influencers who are more familiar with the journey. Sometimes when our practice seems meaningless, we gain perspective by reflecting on the lineage that extends from us all the way back to the first-ever meditator(s).

You might find yourself naturally cultivating a deep appreciation for the austerity and profundity of the meditative tradition. That's fine, but also cultivate a sense of belonging to the tradition yourself. In a sense, you aren't really alone as you sit there on your cushion or chair.

Meditation is like a simple seed. But once cracked open, it spills out in raw, untranslated form all the core teachings and techniques of the great wisdom traditions.

This concept has been with me so long I can't say where it came from. I find it the most vivid metaphor for the meditative process, though. Perhaps it sounds grandiose, seeing that most of us come to meditation for more practical reasons, like to de-stress or sleep better.

Don't feel the need to have a "noble" reason for meditating—like to reach enlightenment or find inner peace. Lofty-sounding motivations are no more effective than humble-sounding ones. In fact, the only effective motivations are those you really feel. False motivations will create a false practice, which naturally isn't as strong as a real one.

So go ahead: Be totally real from the very start.

You might have some doubts or skepticism about meditation alongside your interest in trying it. Acknowledge those as well. Be clear on what your reasons and reservations are and record them in your journal. An accurate picture of your true beginner self will be helpful down the road, when you pause and look back on your journey.

Chapter 2

Forever Beginnings

Your journey of many journeys as a forever beginner

The Meditation for Non-Meditators guide approaches meditation practice as a potential adventure, as if you're just having a look around a new place to see what you think—even if it's not your first time meditating.

Practitioners who are forever beginners have "fresh eyes" and fascinating journeys, and they're more likely to uncover their inner riches. As a forever beginner, each return home becomes simpler and sweeter.

The inner toolbox

Now, remember the companion who shows up with a meditation toolbox ready to help you build your practice, fix whatever you break, and continuously redesign your practice as you grow. Imagine that as you watch her work, you learn more about certain meditation tools and what they're good for.

Depending on where you are in your practice, you might even feel like you already have your own meditation toolbox or are starting to compile one. You might already be creatively at work building your practice.

This section is about mastering the technical know-how to build and rebuild as you explore during practice. The more familiar you are with your tools and how to use them in practice (beyond theory), the easier this section will be to read and digest.

Read this section at any point the curiosity strikes you. Warning: It might seem like we're geeking out on meditation. This chapter breaks meditation down into its nerdy, intellectual bits. Meditation, when translated into technical language, can sound like psychobabble at first.

But any part of this section that lights you up like flipping a switch (ding!) will also light up your practice. Feel free to invite it in and see what happens.

Save for later any part that bores you into sleepiness or has you scratching your head in confusion. Trust that the switch will eventually flip, maybe when you least expect it.

Keep coming home to the idea that our ultimate endeavor isn't to become a Master Craftsman of Meditation, but to rest into the natural flow of meditation.

The basic tools and mediums of meditation

Even the simplest meditation practice has at least one tool for you to use, as well as one medium through which your practice occurs. Enter every session of meditation knowing what your tools and mediums are.

These might not be specified at the outset. Not a problem. At any given moment during practice, they're pretty easy to spot.

Here are the basic tools used in most practices. Each moment in practice utilizes at least one of these:

- Mindfulness
- Awareness
- Concentration
- Acceptance
- Inquiry

Here are the mediums through which most practices flow:

- Mind
- Body
- Emotions
- Senses
- Breath

Each moment in practice occurs within at least one of these mediums. All of these combined make up the broader definition of "mind," which encompasses all the phenomena and experiences that occur in our inner world.

Here's how these tools and mediums worktogether.

In one moment of practice, you might be mindful (tool) of the contents of your mind (medium), such as your thoughts.

In another moment, you might be aware (tool) of your body (medium).

And another moment, you might be concentrating (tool) on your breath (medium).

In yet another moment, you might be inquiring into (tool) your emotions (medium).

All forms of meditation utilize the tools of awareness, concentration, and mindfulness. And if the practice goes to any depth, then you're also likely to need the tools of acceptance and inquiry.

In most meditation practices, we're aware of, mindful of, or concentrating on one of the five mediums.

Mindfulness mediums

Mindfulness is being present with what is actually happening in any given moment.

In life, we're mindful of what we think, feel, and do, as well as how we relate to others.

In meditation, we're always mindful of something, like our moment-to-moment experience or our anchor (if one is specified or chosen).

Anchors are specific objects that we are mindful of or concentrate on during practice. Usually, an anchor is the thing we continually return focus to, such as the breath, a mantra, a body sensation, or an image we visualize in our mind's eye or rest our gaze upon.

In both meditation and life, what we experience about ourselves and our world comes to us as:

- Thoughts (mind as medium)
- Sensations (body as medium)
- Feelings, moods (emotions as medium)
- Perceptions (senses as medium)
- Breath

Thankfully, we're not fully mindful of all of these all day, every day. (Just imagine how exhausting life would be, and how muddy our picture of reality would appear.)

Just as thankfully, we're not able to be 100% mindful of just one thing while the rest of the world is 100% shut out. (That would be dangerous, for one thing.)

Instead of the all or nothing approach, we use mindfulness in a more balanced way. We direct our mindfulness towards something, observing what it does while still having some awareness of other things going on in the background.

What we find to be real in any given moment depends on what we are and aren't mindful of, as well as which medium our mindfulness is occurring through.

Let's return to the train conductor in order to explore how our version of reality is determined by what we're aware of. Imagine the conductor's view as the train rolls through the busy city and then into the desert.

If the conductor is overwhelmed with thoughts (like financial worries, for example) his experience of driving the train through the city and the desert might be overshadowed by thinking about how much money's in his bank account, when he'll get his next paycheck, what bills are piling up, how he's going to ask his friend for a loan, how he'll explain everything to his spouse, and what he might do next.

Now imagine meeting the conductor at the train station afterwards. As he steps out of the train you say, "How was the trip?" He might say, "Really stressful," barely remembering the city and desert. His thoughts are overshadowing his senses.

Now imagine the conductor is an aesthete, with a taste for beauty and sensory-indulgence. As the train rolls through the city, his eyes feast upon all the glitter, noise, movement, and modernity. His senses are working overtime to drink it all in.

Then, as the city fades into a wide desert panoramic view, he gasps. His eyes blink, adjusting to the vast open space.

He takes a deep breath, soothed by the quiet. His eyes sweep through the vastness searching for an object.

"Hmmm, nothing ... nothing ... then...."Ah, a deer on the horizon. Amazing!"

This conductor is still having thoughts, but the sight and sound of the journey pouring through his senses dominates his reality. His thoughts are actually supporting his senses, helping to make reality even more meaningful and real to him.

Now imagine this aesthete conductor actually has the same financial problems as the worried one. Their financial reality is the same, but their versions of "what happened on the train ride through the city and the desert" are quite different. Yet each version is equally real to each conductor.

Now imagine these two train conductors as one person who has made the same city-to-desert journey two different times, experiencing the two different moods on each trip. The reality of the first trip was stressful, while the second was a feast for the senses.

So it is with meditation. If we choose to be mindful of body sensation, our experience of reality will be different than if we're mindful of emotions. The medium is the message. What message we hear (or what version of reality) depends on what medium is transmitting the message.

But there's more.

Mind, body, emotions, senses, and breath aren't actually separate from one another. They are all interlinked in the web of personal experience. The breath moving through the body creates sensations we can feel, sound we can hear, and emotions we experience. When we become emotionally overwhelmed, our breath, body, mind, and sensory perception change dramatically.

Our experience of mind, body, emotions, sensation, and breath is forever changing. We can practice the same meditation a dozen days and have a dozen unique experiences.

Why does all this matter?

When we find ourselves at a crossroads, we see we have choices in which direction to go—the way of mind, body, emotions, sensation, breath, or combinations of these.

At this point, we see our freedom and the responsibility required to skillfully make the most of it.

We're responsible for where our mindfulness goes as we practice and the reality our choices help create.These choices shape our practice and influence our lives.

The choices we make about which mediums we're mindful of directly influence how well we "get along" with our practice.Direct your mindfulness according to what supports your needs and intentions.

Which medium is the right one for us will become apparent over time.The more we practice through different mediums (just like taking different routes), the more we begin to find the way that's right for us.

Honesty is one of the most helpful tools in determining which way is right for us.

One of meditation's superhero powers is nurturing honesty. It really can be that companion who sets you straight when you're kidding yourself. "Tough love" isn't fun to receive, but deep down we know that the truest friends are those who lovingly call us out.

An honest meditation practice can be this true friend.

Let's now take a closer look at mind, body, emotions, senses, and breath.

Mind in meditation: Patterns of thought

Unlike other animals, humans have special inherent mental abilities— thinking, reasoning, imagining, and planning, just to name a few. Our minds weave thought patterns and narratives to create realities.

Our way of perceiving, collecting, storing, deleting, processing, synthesizing, transforming, and transferring information is in some ways analogous to a computer hard drive.

The mind is a database containing myriad forms of knowledge, memory, wisdom, and mind stuff, with the capability to process all of the data.

Our mind manipulates, transforms, and creates data.

As the mind processes, it creates patterns allowing us to use the data faster, more efficiently, and with deeper meaning.

These patterns become ingrained in us, making up our personality, life story, routines, relationships, aspirations, and creations. We use these patterns so instinctively that we lose the sense of having the option to put them aside.

It's not so much that we choose this; it just happens as a part of our development. Learning behavior patterns is a big part of early childhood development.

This pattern-making tendency is an amazing gift, but it also has limits. After all, the patterns aren't foolproof. They can be unreliable, inappropriate, or faulty. Sometimes, we half-consciously continue a bad pattern because it's easier than making a new one.

How we use patterns (and how they use us) becomes more apparent during meditation. While practicing, we see our patterns for what they are, as well as how they affect our behavior, our lives, and other people's lives.

Here are a few patterns of mind you might discover in your meditation practice. Notice which ones recur the most and record them in your journal.

- Thinking
- Mental chattering
- Daydreaming
- Judging
- Planning
- Rehearsing
- Remembering
- Contrasting and comparing
- Counting and measuring
- Denying and revising reality
- Doubting, questioning, and being skeptical

Now that we've established the pattern-making aspect of mind, let's look at how basic functions of mind help us in meditation practice.

Mind in meditation: Awareness, concentration, and mindfulness

Two of the most common aspects of mind that we work with in meditation are awareness and concentration. Awareness is direct perception of what's happening in the present moment. Concentration is the ability to remain focused on an object or anchor for a sustained period of time.

Awareness and concentration can be wider or narrower. However, concentration helps us narrow our focus while awareness is most helpful when focus opens to expansion. Both awareness and concentration fall under the umbrella of mindfulness.

All three work together as intertwining pathways of effort.

Here's an example of how this unfolds:

If we focus on a single mantra, our concentration is continually narrowing away from distraction and towards the mantra.

We are most mindful of the mantra, but also aware of other things (noises, for example) in the background. We're still aware of the noise, but less mindful of it.

If our focus opens wider to take in other things, then we let them become equal to the mantra in our awareness—these can be noises + thoughts + body sensation. We're mindful of more things but are concentrating less.

Awareness is more open-ended.

Another example. Imagine you're practicing concentration, when you're startled by a sudden disruption.

You gasp, and then recognize the disruption.

Your awareness opens to identify the offending disruption.

Then, you're aware of being distracted, plus any reactions you're having.

You're mindful of needing to return to practice.

You begin the return to your concentration by re-focusing on your anchor. But...

Again and again, you're continually distracted by the memory of the disruption and your reactions to it.

You're also aware of new reactions that arise (like frustration), as well as any other experiences you're starting to feel (like physical discomfort), while staying mindful of your overall process of returning to concentration.

Gradually, your focus begins to narrow.

Eventually, the distraction, reactions, and discomfort fall away and concentration returns.

Huge leaps in understanding and insight can be made after a session by reviewing the interplay of awareness, concentration, and mindfulness. Record these insights in your journal. Avoid obsessing over how aware, focused, or mindful you were or should have been.

Mind in meditation: Acceptance

Both true beginnings and forever beginnings hinge on acceptance.

True beginners accept that they get distracted often or tend to lose their way in unfamiliar situations. Forever beginners accept that no matter how seasoned their practice is, they too can become distracted and confused— not to mention that what they think are breakthrough insights are often later revealed as illusions.

Acceptance can easily be mistaken for compromise, but it actually grants us the power to be present. We're truly present when we allow conditions to "just be," rather than reacting or trying to control them.

Also, acceptance shouldn't be mistaken for false positivity. Least of all is it pretending to endorse something we actively dislike.

Naturally, we dislike that we easily become distracted. But we accept it, refocus, and move on. To get wrapped up in frustration means sacrificing the power of our presence.

Let's use the example of repetitive sound to look at how this works in meditation. We can explore the sound because we accept that the sound is there. Not accepting the sound would generate reactions like:
- I hate this sound.
- I'm bored of this sound and want something new.
- Or, I like the sound and want it to return now that it's gone.

These reactions are fine in one sense, but are overshadowing our practice of being mindful of sound. So, while we're having those reactions, we aren't entirely present in our practice.

Reactionary moments are inevitable during meditation, which is good news on the acceptance front. Once we realize we're reacting, we can accept this and simply move on.

Acceptance isn't weak, but rather powerful passivity. It builds meditative muscle, which then builds a stronger ability to accept.

Mind in meditation: Inquiry

Throughout life, we're often advised not to dig too deep into anything and to accept surface-truth as reality. Try as we might to ignore deeper truth, it has a way of revealing itself.

As our experiences flow along, we can't help but learn more about them. We start to recognize patterns. Then we see each iteration of the pattern, spotting any unique variations or transformations over time.

In meditation, when we concentrate on an anchor over time, we naturally begin to see deeper into its essential nature. Also, we're drawn to the more subtle experience and mystery of empty spaces in our consciousness, like the way we're curious about what's on the other side of a passing train. We narrow our eyes and focus on the fleeting gaps between the train cars.

Both examples in the previous paragraph are meditative inquiry, or the ability to see vividly into the nature of experiences and objects. However, meditative inquiry isn't meant to form rigid opinions about what things are—quite the opposite.

Inquiry is an effort and a tool. If it's introduced too soon into a beginner's practice, it can be confusing and distracting. There's a fine distinction between getting caught up in the details of something versus looking deeper into patterns and essential nature.

During practice, if you find yourself engaged in inquiry into something other than your anchor, consider moving on, staying with your practice and your anchor.

Acknowledge that you found inquiry and would like to explore it later. You might make note of the experience in your journal.

If you're curious about how inquiry functions in practice, read on.

Meditative inquiry is like a laser beam that illuminates the temporary, changeable, and conditional nature of things in our consciousness, as well as in our outer world. Patterns emerge from darkness and dullness. We watch them shift, transform, fall apart, disappear, and reappear.

For example, imagine your practice involves listening to sound in a fairly quiet room. Your lens of awareness responds to the quiet by opening wide to capture even the subtlest sounds in the distance.

Then a repetitive sound arises, such as a dripping faucet. At first you're aware of a single sound, then a pattern of sound. As you continue to focus on the sound pattern, you're inquiring into the pattern itself.

You're not looking for anything, but you start to hear the drip's subtle variations in tone, volume, and rhythm. You're not forming an opinion of the pattern, but you're listening to its changeable nature momenttomoment until it transforms entirely, goes away, or is drowned out by something else in the sound landscape. If we aren't experienced at inquiry, the sound can become a distraction—even a source of frustration.

Inquiry—like awareness, concentration, and mindfulness—is something we carry from practice into life and bring from life into practice.

Inquiry also can be a mediation practice in itself, where we focus our intention on looking deeper into experiences by continually asking questions and/or listening for guidance from our intuition. These questions serve as anchors. But inquiry isn't about finding an answer in the absolute sense, though we may fashion an answer from what we discover during inquiry.

For the sake of clarity, let's review this once more.

> Awareness, concentration, inquiry, and acceptance are the primary tools used in meditation. They're naturally intertwined.

> It's possible to be so caught up in our minds that we aren't aware of our body. But our body is still host to the functioning of the other three mediums. On the flip side, in moments of intense pleasure and pain, our minds, senses, and emotions are still at work, though all we feel is the power of the sensation that captures our bodies.

Awareness, concentration, inquiry, and acceptance aren't just tools for working with thoughts. They're our tools when working with the body, senses, and emotions as well.

The body: A location, map, and language

The body is the place where all our experiences happen. We are embodied beings, which means everything we think, feel, sense, and imagine—no matter how abstract—is somehow rooted in the body. This is good or bad news, depending on how connected your awareness is to your body.

For this reason, the body is an excellent medium to work with in meditation. In fact, the body is an essential medium. All mindfulness needs to be directed through the body at some point. Otherwise, the body starts to break down. Not only that—we can become "floaty," disembodied, and ungrounded.

In other words, the other three mediums for mindfulness inevitably include the body as part of the process.

What we actually find inside bodily experience during meditation is a larger landscape containing the mini landscapes of mind, emotion, and the senses. We also encounter an actual map of the landscape of the body. This isn't a metaphoric map, but a literal one that the mind reads in order for the body to function. It's called the Mind-Body Map.

We use our body as a vehicle to get us around, like a workhorse to get us what we want, and even as an object of vanity. None of these are examples of bodily awareness.

This is why it's dangerous to live out our days completely entangled in thought patterns, swept away by emotions, drunk on our sensory indulgence to the point that we've lost awareness of our body.

Fortunately, there are many ways to increase bodily awareness through meditation. The most common practices are:
- Body scanning
- Moving awareness through points of the body
- Listening to sensations in the body as a language
- Moving meditations

Body scanning. Just as the title indicates, this is moving awareness through the body like a scanner, connecting to certain areas or the whole body in a linear fashion. Visual people will somehow "see" the scanner, perhaps as a light, while sensing people will internally "feel" where the scanner is at any given moment.

Moving awareness through body points. This method is similar to scanning, except that the awareness can jump from one place to another rather than flowing linearly. When moving through points, the attention rests for a moment on a part of the body, and then skips to another. For example, our attention might move from the head to the feet, then the whole front of the body to the back of the body.

Listening to body sensation. Painful and pleasurable sensations exist in the body to help us take care of it physically and have the best life possible. Sensation is the language of the body and it's full of reliable information. Listening to body sensation with the same level of sensitivity, curiosity, and intimacy as we listen to the words of a close friend is a satisfying, healing, and grounding practice. But first we have to learn the language and develop an ear for it. Meditation is the way to become familiar with patterns and nuances of body sensation. Once we're familiar, the intimacy only deepens.

Moving meditation. Meditation doesn't just occur in stillness. So much of what we do everyday involves movement. So learning to maintain awareness during mobility is important in bringing our practice off the cushion and into our lives. Moving meditation is meditating while moving. Obvious enough. But meditative movement is something else. Meditative movement prioritizes movement over meditation. We're moving more mindfully, but not fully meditating.

The weather of emotions: Deluge and drought

Emotions come and go like the weather. They can be strong and torrential, weak and patchy, or even seemingly absent. They have conditions, tones, and textures such as wet, dry, windy, moderate, and sunny.

Some traditions consider emotions a part of the mind because thoughts and feelings are so inherently linked—and because both are so subjective. Emotions move like thoughts do.But in the case of stronger gusts of emotion, their movement is often more apparent. Like thoughts, emotions tend to form patterns—some of which become habit and create realities, and some of which we live out as absolute truth.

We don't perceive through our emotions or our thoughts, but both translate what we perceive into a reality that we can articulate as "what is happening right now." Or, "here's what I saw yesterday...." What actually happens in a moment is completely distinct from what we think and feel about what actually happens. Yet, what we think and feel become our reality.

Deluge

Strong emotions of any kind can sweep away or overpower the most logical, sober attempts to remain mindful because emotions are inherently reactionary. Meditation can be quite challenging or seem entirely impossible during strong emotional reactions.

I know because I've been there. I came to yoga and meditation as a way to deal with emotional anxiety and stress. For years, a strong emotional gust could rise up in me and blow out like a tiny candle months of mindfulness. Or so it seemed. I didn't know it then, but my mindfulness muscle got stronger every time the candle was squelched.

To this day, I'm still passionate and vividly emotional. I'm far from having perfect emotional pitch.But thanks to meditation and mindfulness, I've come to not only respect my emotions, but also consider them one of my most worthwhile offerings to the world.

When overwhelmed by emotional deluge, we can choose to:
- Use the emotion in practice
- Place our attention elsewhere until the deluge subsides

(For more about feeling emotionally overwhelmed, see "Meditating through life's rough patches.")

Use emotions in practice. We can center our practice around emotions as they occur, allowing ourselves to be mindful of them. We can go one step further and use them as an anchor by continually returning our attention to our emotions, even when something else becomes more prominent.

Either way, our mindfulness of emotions might open up to inquiry. We might find ourselves penetrating into an emotion and discovering the deeper layers—like what the emotion is connected to, how it operates, or where there are subtle changes in tone and texture.

During challenging emotional times, this is the path of least resistance. If we're tired, we can relax effort and just watch emotions bluster through, transform, and finally die down. It's like sitting in a storm without shelter, letting yourself get soaked and feel it all. Passive as it may seem, this approach requires skill and radical degrees of tolerance. Patience is essential when the emotions don't go away as soon as we'd like.

Also, we have to be careful not to prolong the emotional period as observers. We can get so used to certain emotional patterns that we may think we're passively observing, when in fact we're sustaining the pattern or even creating one in a state of indulgence.

Place attention elsewhere repeatedly. This also requires patience and persistence. Every time you find yourself completely preoccupied by emotions, return your attention to the anchor. Mantra tends to be as effective an anchor as any during these times—so people say. Mantra doesn't work so well with my emotional patterns, though. I feel like the mantra tries to compete with and drown out the emotion by internally "yelling" the word or phrase. Watching the breath is my chosen approach.

Drought

There are moments when we feel no emotion at all, or the emotions are so indescribable that it seems like nothing is there. The pleasant form of this might be emotional spaciousness, when the empty space feels like a wide-open area that allows us freedom and lightness. The more unpleasant end of the drought spectrum might be emotional numbness during an emergency or trauma, when we'd normally feel a deluge.

Working with emotional drought in meditation usually means choosing another medium. Often the mind can be a helpful medium through which we can do some detective work to uncover why our emotions have dried up. The mind will often reveal the exact reason we aren't feeling anything.

A common revelation is that the mind has become so dominant, it has convinced us that our emotions aren't to be trusted or that they don't contain any insight. But emotions are often a more trustworthy form of insight than thought-generated insight.

Feeling-tones

Moderate emotional weather offers a different array of meditative possibilities. One of the most common is mindfulness of "feeling-tones".

We used a storm to represent the strong emotions in the example above. Now let's imagine a light rain that vacillates between a mist and a drizzle. The feeling-tone of mist might register as soft, sweet, and lightly refreshing in a warm climate, or clammy and damp in a colder one.

As the rain becomes heavier, the tone changes from less soft to slightly agitating in a warm climate. Shivers run up your spine as the rain runs down your skin, and the experience moves into unpleasant territory.

As the displeasure increases, our reactions become more important. Reactions such as "Ugh, I hate this!" lend power to the emotion, which can seem to grow bigger than ourselves and eventually overwhelm us.

On the other hand, observing displeasure directly and mindfully by surrounding it with our awareness tends to contain it, preventing it from overwhelming us.

Pleasurable feeling-tones are like any other positive experience during practice. We want them to last. Once they stop, we long to recreate them. But try as we might, the feeling is never exactly the same. Enjoy pleasant feeling-tones, inquire into them if you like, but don't try to hang onto them. Allow them to come and go freely, just like unpleasant feeling-tones.

Emotional mind, emotional body:

The bottom line when working with emotions and feeling-tones is to notice the way they mirror in the mind (the emotional mind) and in the body (the emotional body).

Left unchecked, many (if not all) emotions will have an automatic, corresponding thought that occurs along with it, as well as an automatic, corresponding body sensation.

The mind narrates and builds judgments alongside emotion, whereas the body echoes the emotion with a physical sensation. Listen to the body's response to emotions rather than the mind's. The mind might be a useful tool for finding the reason we feel (or don't feel) a certain emotion. But the body's response can tell us so much more. Think about it. The mind can lie quite easily. The body, not so much.

The traditional meditation practice of Lovingkindness is the finest example of inquiring into emotions and feeling-tones while listening to the body. In Lovingkindness, we focus our attention on our chest area, the heart-center, and watch sensations arise as we wish ourselves and others well in life. Lovingkindness has been treasured through the ages because it heals emotional wounds, grounds our emotional awareness in our bodies, and reveals to us who we are on otherwise very deep and hidden emotional levels.

The realm of the senses: Abstinence and indulgence

We are mindful of the senses to some degree—whether we're instructed to keep sensory information in the background, or to focus on a specific sense like listening to sounds come and go.

Meditation instructions sometimes advise "sensory abstinence," or letting go of outside sensory information (or "internalizing the senses") for the sake of turning inward. Practicing letting the senses go, or letting them fall to the background, doesn't mean we're building a wall against them. We're usually still noticing sensory information. We're just not allowing it to dominate our awareness or set off chains of thought and emotion.

Examples of letting go of the senses are:

- Mantra practice
- Internal body scans (not using body sensation)
- Mindfulness of thought and internal chatter

When we're encouraged to incorporate the senses, or even a single sense, we perceive sensory information coming and going. If we're using only one sense as an anchor, we avoid allowing other senses to dominate. In all cases, we still don't allow the senses, even our anchor, to set off chains of thought and emotion.

Examples of focusing on one or more of these senses are:

- Gazing at a candle (using sight only and a single object as an anchor)
- Sky-gazing (using sight only and multiple objects as anchors, such as clouds, birds, or colors)
- Listening to sound (using sound only and multiple objects as anchors)
- Focusing on the breath (using multiple senses, such as sound, body sensation, or touch—and potentially smell)

The medium is the message

Perhaps you recognize the title of this section as a quote from the late Marshall McLuhan, the philosopher and theorist who some say predicted the future of the worldwide web. McLuhan's original idea of "medium as message" was in reference to the nature of advertising, especially via television.

The "medium as message" idea can be applied universally. I'm using it here as a modern way of characterizing mind and its unfolding through thought, sensation, emotion, and perception.

The medium we practice through will affect what we experience and learn, how we grow, what we believe, and what we do.

Always be conscious of where your information is coming from and what it's flowing through (the medium). All information is encoded with messages.

There are myriad ways to use these mediums (combinations of mind, body, emotions, senses, and breath) in each situation according to your level of practice and what your intentions are.

One factor to consider is how easy and natural versus how challenging and unpredictable you want your practice to be. More about this:

Simple and natural:

If you want to keep it simple, either because you're a true beginner or because you find a lot of meaning in simple practices, use a medium that's natural for your given situation. For example, if you're practicing in a jungle or forest where there are many sounds, fragrances, and sensory experiences, you might choose the senses as your medium.

Another way to keep it simple is to choose a medium you're naturally pre-disposed to, such as mind as medium—if the mind is where your attention is naturally drawn.

More challenging and unpredictable:

To make practice more interesting, challenging, or deep, choose a medium that isn't as natural in a given situation, such as mind as medium (or watching thoughts) while in a jungle or another location offering lots of sensory information.

Or perhaps consider a medium you are less predisposed to. For example, if your attention is naturally drawn to your thoughts and is barely present in the body, practice mindfulness of the body (or watching body sensations come and go.)

Chapter 3

The Glow and Flow of Insight

Early insight

In meditation, as in life, insight doesn't hit us on the head like a coconut falling from a tree.

Insight—along with awareness, concentration, mindfulness, inquiry, and acceptance—is our birthright. However, it needs to be constantly cultivated.

Awareness, concentration, mindfulness, inquiry, and acceptance are accessible, practical tools that even true beginners can handle right away. Everyday survival requires these basic tools, especially awareness and concentration. Life gradually etches awareness and concentration into habit. We're often able to apply them effortlessly.

Meditative insight, however, isn't a tool and can't really be "handled." More slippery than awareness and concentration, meditative insight can be difficult to recognize if you don't know what to look for.

Furthermore, meditative insight usually arises on its own, once we've gotten past frequent distraction.

So what is meditative insight and how do we cultivate it?

Meditative insight begins after mindfulness starts to flow unceasingly and often lasts only a brief period of time.

Meditative insight is different than the intellectual insight we encounter as part of our learning process. Intellectual insight is often more specific: A crystallization, "aha" moment, or conclusion that we can directly apply to our lives. Usually, even the most profound intellectual insight usually can be articulated as a nugget of wisdom.

Meditative insight is more open-ended: More process than result, and more of a movement than anything you can hang onto.

I'm not sure that meditative insight is even wisdom, although it definitely nurtures wise thinking and living.

Often referred to as "flow," meditative insight is an experience of ease and natural fluidity in mindful life as well as in meditation practice.

We're hardwired to experience the natural flow of insight. Seeds of meditative insight are intact in us at birth. We're designed to walk around on normal days relatively at ease and "lit up" by insight.

Furthermore, we're meant to experience ease and insight even when we're confused or in a stressful situation. We're designed to figure life out without freaking out—in real-time or, in some cases, in hindsight.

Yet, the world of distraction we grow up in turns our focus from this natural state of glow and flow. We're taught not to trust ourselves. Many distractions—such as advertising, drugs, and expensive possessions—are designed to dazzle us, sometimes even outshine us, with their bright artificial light. Furthermore, we begin to trust The Experts who create, produce, and sell distraction.

Some of us grow to depend on this artificial light to illuminate our life's path, and eventually maybe even believe we're in darkness without the artificial illumination.

The good news is that one of the primary reasons we practice meditation is to rediscover, reclaim, and reignite our natural insight.

Again, let's return to the train cars.

Imagine each car is a thought. When we aren't mindful of our thoughts, we're captivated by them. Being captivated by a single train of thought is like being trapped inside a single train car.

The view from the inside of the train car is quite limited. We have no way to stand back and see the cars or the spaces between them.

We can only go where the train carries us.

Once we separate ourselves from the train, we can stand back and watch the cars roll by, seeing each one distinctly along with the spaces between.

When we're locked into our thoughts and locked out of our insight, our view is limited in a similar way. Until we find the way to get off the thought-train, we have no choice about where it takes us.

Mindfulness of thought (or sounds, or body sensation) allows enough distance to be aware of the thoughts' movements and distinct qualities. We see one thought after another roll by, and sometimes penetrate the spaces between.

We see each thought as a distinct part of our mind, like each car as a part of the train.

Early insight is the mind witnessing its own workings with awareness that the workings are separate from the witnessing.

Read that last sentence again if you need to, then pause and reflect. You've experienced this in your life at least once or twice, if not many times over, right?

I often take a moment or two during the centering phase of my practice to feel this separation. I move between feeling the experience of practice (what's going on), then feeling myself as a witness to the experience (the being who's watching, listening, etc. to what's going on) and then back to feeling the experience and workings of the mind.

True beginners often find this practice helpful towards the end of a session, or any time in practice they feel centered enough to explore movement between these two layers of consciousness.

In the early phases of insight, your realizations flow and glow. They appear direct, clean, and pristine.

You might not have any words to express the experience afterwards in your journal. Do your best. Draw them or sing them as sounds into your phone. Whatever works.

Maybe you describe the way you feel afterwards rather than fumbling with an accurate portrayal of the experience itself.

Deepening insight

Record your impressions somehow—not because you'll someday make perfect sense of your meditative insight, but because attempting to represent it consciously helps you deepen your connection to insight-consciousness.

Your insight will continue to deepen. Life will get deeper as well—more mysterious, more difficult to describe—in a good way. Other people will notice your deepening. They'll compliment you on the profoundness of your insight and seek you out for it. Or, they'll notice you look different—that you actually have a glow, and seem more at ease or more self-confident.

In your own internal experience, deepening of insight is like this: Experience of the mind and its workings are devoid of a single, united self.

This experience of the mind working constantly changes.

Every moment seems to invent itself, then eventually transforms or disappears.

If this sounds lofty, think about it in terms of the train, which also doesn't have a single united self. We say it does. We have an idea of a train; we call it "train." But really, it's our mind that turns this collection of cars into a "train."

Don't believe it? Imagine the train in pieces at the junkyard, strewn around amongst other pieces of junk metal. No more train, no way to tell which pieces were or weren't part of the train.

Some of the metal goes to recycling, blended with other metal bits and made into different objects, maybe cars instead of train cars. You wouldn't look at one of these new cars and think, "That was a train". Other parts of the train might be abandoned in the junkyard forever, left to rust in the rain.

We want to ride safely on the train, so we necessarily see it as a solid, permanent, real thing. That's fine, and it's wise. The same goes for thoughts. We need to believe in them in order to bring them to life as concrete form and action, but we also need to acknowledge that thoughts are creations that can be recycled, abandoned to rust, or just left to flow along and do what they do.

The more insight we have, the less whole, solid, and real our mind seems. Insight highlights the impermanence of mind. But don't worry, our minds aren't going to unravel and decompose because we have a moment of insight now and then.

In fact, our relationship to our mind is strengthened by insight into its impermanence. We reclaim our power over mind and begin to use mind appropriately, rather than mind using us.

The mind using us is like the train driving the conductor. We have an expression for this—we call it a runaway train! A stressed out mind is like a runaway train dragging the conductor along a destructive path.

Back to deepening of insight. Once we know what meditative insight is like, we begin to recognize it when it lights up and begins to flow. (For more about deepening insight and practice, see "What to do when shifts happen.")

Flow of insight sounds groovy and amazing. We think, "Yes! How do I get there?"

The truth is less glamorous.

While insight is actually flowing, we're at ease. Once the flow ceases, or just before it begins, we can bump up against obstacles and get gummed up in grief.

The broader experience of earlier forms of insight and its ever-changing nature can be quite uncomfortable—even painful.

This earlier insight period is often a process of reckoning—of old stuff working itself out. We're haunted by howls of our old habits that are afraid of change, or soon-to-be-obsolete methods of control not wanting to let go of us.

You might experience wanting to fidget, change your posture, or end the practice early. Hold steady. You're experiencing the consequences of being on the brink of transformation.

More about holding steady at the brink in the next section.

Effortless insight

Effortless insight begins after insight has started to flow for longer durations. It occurs after we feel the relief of having entered an empty space.

Just before entering an empty space, or during the first moments of entry—before resting into the relief of its flow—the discomfort, doubt, or displeasure we experience is a gift disguised as a shock. We practice holding steady and moving through. The gift becomes clear on the other side, if we make it there.

Holding steady through the crazy phases of deepening insight might seem counter-intuitive. The key to moving through the apparent craziness? Mindfulness.

Holding steady while remaining mindful of discomfort will eventually dissolve the discomfort.

Your mindfulness eventually drains the discomfort of its power.

You stop believing the inner hype.

You see the man behind the curtain.

You struggle as you move into another layer of consciousness, but eventually rest into your own natural meditative power.

Movement into a newer, less familiar empty space is like the conductor entering an unfamiliar terrain or one that has changed drastically since his last trip through. The first moments of entry are a shock. He struggles to maintain composure as his senses try to grasp the situation. He feels edgy; maybe his control of the train is challenged, but he eventually regains it.

Remaining mindful of a seeming threat during practice is key for this reason: Doing the opposite—ending practice or suppressing feelings, such as fear of a perceived threat—only prolongs and intensifies the power of that perceived threat. Growth is halted during these moments.

Here's another special feature of effortless insight. We get to enjoy it while we're there.

Earlier versions of insight are less conscious. We often realize insight has occurred only after it's passed.

As the relief of effortless insight sets in, we feel our sense of discord and separation lift.

Our mind flows along automatically and lucidly.

We are free of delight as well as displeasure.

We realize we're deep in empty space.

We're at the peak of inner freedom.

If you find yourself in this sublime place, flow on in your effortlessness for as long as it lasts. If your timer goes off and you can still maintain the effortless flow, keep going.

Feel this freedom as yourself just being you—beyond the power of words and concepts.

Savor a sublime practice like this, and afterwards reflect upon the practice as well as your overall journey. You've travelled from the true beginnings of trying to master tools (awareness, concentration, and acceptance) into the forever beginnings of searching for more pure experiences through the mediums (mind, body, emotions, senses, and breath.)

In effortless insight, you are simple and full human embodiment.

You have no sense of separation between the mediums of mind, body, emotions, senses, and breath.

You have no sense of tools, no need for tools.

Nirvana

Somewhere beyond effortless insight is Nirvana. We've come this far, so we should briefly reflect on what Nirvana is like.

For the sake of clarity, let's imagine for a moment that meditation is a linear process with an actual ending. If that were the case, Nirvana would be the result or reward cheering for you at the finish line of meditation.

Like a river flows into the ocean, or a pathway opens into a vast field, effortless insight opens up into the infinite space of Nirvana.

Most of us experience only the briefest flashes of nirvana (with a lowercase "n"—that's mini-nirvana, quasi-nirvana, or nano-nirvana). No compromise is being made. Make no mistake; a little nirvana goes a long, long way.

When in a state of Nirvana (uppercase "N"), you're something other than your normal self.

Nirvana is completely beyond common reality, as well as the words that shape common reality.

The word Nirvana means "non-burning," a state when our desire—and all that our desire creates—is absolutely burned out.

We're not wishing for anything or pursuing anything. We're not averse to anything, or letting go of anything. We aren't in a state of transformation or avoiding change. There's no flow. We're just resting in pristine consciousness.

(This is the best words can do to describe what Nirvana is like.)

Of course, meditation isn't a linear process and Nirvana isn't like a train arriving to a destination. Trying to attain Nirvana, or trying too hard to arrive at any level of enlightenment through meditation, isn't going to be helpful.

Nirvana in meditation is like the idea of Perfection. It's best treated as a direction to travel towards. But don't count on getting there. Even if you arrive at Nirvana, the train might roll through so quickly, you could blink and miss the whole thing.

Chapter 4

Horizons Everywhere, Forever

Now, let's pause again and reflect.

We've moved through the beginnings of awareness, concentration, and mindfulness. We went onward through the mind, body, emotions, senses, and breath as mediums through which experience flows. We continued on to insight, finally arriving at Nirvana.

Meditation is a journey with pit stops along the way. We move through walls and other blocks as we grow.

We set off in a certain direction, but there's no ultimate destination.

We think of meditation as a linear journey in order to make sense of it. Really though, meditation is more like sinking in and out of layers—circling, zigzagging, spiraling up and down—moving through them in all kinds of ways.

We know what meditation is in theory way before we're able to actualize them in practice for more than a few moments at a time. We need to be reminded again and again in action what we already know in theory.

This is why we call ourselves forever beginners.

Life is rich and diverse, so there's no way to list all the experiences you might encounter as you meditate. Practice gets smoother and easier, then seemingly bumpier and more challenging.

Sometimes your practice needs routine, rigor, and discipline. Other times practice calls for experimentation, spontaneity, and wildness.

There are periods of blandness and boredom where disappointment starts to creep in.Then, all of a sudden, practice is like a rollercoaster or a Tilt-a-Whirl.

You are deepening and growing.

This closing section is devoted to highlighting some of the most common situations you're likely to find along your journey, if you haven't found them already.

The nitty-gritty of meditation-mapping

Below are nine steps to guide you in making your own practice plan.

1. Don't overthink or postpone making a plan by waiting for the "right time" or the "right set of conditions." Skip and save for later any consideration you find yourself over-thinking. (Remember: Perfectionism can be a form of procrastination. Besides, the best time to meditate is when things are far from perfect.)

2. Choose a good place to practice—preferably one that's comfortable, safe, and quiet.

3. Designate the duration of your trial period, or how long you're willing to try meditation. At least a week is recommended. One month is better, six months is ideal. This is a consideration many of us brush over, but it prevents you from expecting too much out of your first few practices and instead lets you focus on getting focused.

4. Fix a time of day for your daily practice and stick to it as best you can. (If you miss a session, don't worry. Any time you feel like practicing is a good time.)

5. Designate how long each session will be and use a timer. At least 1-5 minutes is recommended. Choose a length that feels challenging but reasonable. Don't be tempted to overreach.

   One minute of good practice is better than none. There's a one-minute practice in the Meditation for Non-Meditators guide called "Most of a Minute" that can be done anywhere, anytime and doesn't require a timer. For anything longer than a minute, use a timer with a bell so you're not repeatedly distracted by clock-watching.

6. Stick to the designated amount of practice time in each session. Doubtful or disappointing days are actually the best days to practice because we break through much of the resistance embedded in our past conditioning. Any amount of time—even a few seconds of taking conscious deep breaths—is more beneficial than you might think.

7. After a week, consider increasing your practice time if you discover you can explore for longer.

8. Keep a journal or some kind of record in writing, video, or audio—or even draw pictures if that works for you. Note what's prominent in your experience while meditating. Other things you might take note of:

   - How long you practice

   - The quality of your attention

   - Emotions and sensations that arise

   - Challenges you meet

   - Experiences you enjoy

   - Any signs of progress

   - How you feel afterwards

   Also, record any rough ideas or vague inklings. Represent them any way you can, even in simple, crude forms. These inklings will clarify over time into special pearls of wisdom.

9. Once your trial period is complete, pause and reflect. How have you changed? What have you learned? What about the experience stands out? What do you need to work on? Be as thorough as possible.

These nine considerations will help you map out your overall journey. Not only will you know where you're going, but you'll also be way more clear about why and how you want to explore meditation. You're journey will be more meaningful and fun because you took the time to get clear about your purpose.

Also, each session of practice is a journey unto itself. To help each session be as meaningful and fun as possible, take some time to prepare. Launch your practice as consciously as possible.

Before beginning each session, consider these things:

1. Body position and posture. Most important is comfort. Sit in a chair if sitting on the floor is distracting. The position you're most comfortable in is the one you'll have the best practice in. If need be, lie down.

2. Breath. All types of meditation should have some consideration of breath. Many begin meditation with attention to breathing. Some focus only on the breath the whole practice.

3. Thoughts. They're always going to be present. Their nature is to appear and dazzle. Meditation is NOT about getting rid of them. If you're particularly prone to thoughts during practice, you might use them as a focus rather than disregarding them. Reference "Showgirl Thoughts" in the Meditation for Non-Meditators guide.

If you're instructed in a particular practice to let go of thoughts, don't worry if they make a recurring appearance. Don't try to kick them out of the meditation arena, and don't wrestle with them either. If you have them in a headlock, they're not going anywhere!

Continually return your attention to your object of focus during your practice, knowing that with every return to focus, the pattern of distraction is erased a little bit more. This object of focus is called the anchor, because it literally grounds your practice.

Embarrassing, kooky, and amazing

At first, it might seem like nothing is happening in practice.

However, once we're quiet and still enough to notice subtlety, it can get pretty lively. We might start noticing some odd things and wonder what they mean.

It's normal to have certain unusual experiences. Some linger while others pop in from nowhere, never to return again.

On some level, we want to be interested in everything we experience during practice. We're watching layers of things come and go.

Sometimes when unusual experiences occur, our tendency is to delve into them and try to figure them out. We wonder if there's a problem, or the opposite—if we're about to become enlightened!

Here are some of the most common oddball experiences and how to work with them. Let's start with things that might seem kooky or embarrassing:

1. Falling asleep. This is very common and generally nothing to worry about. Although if you're in a group, snoring isn't going to make you any meditation friends. If your sleeping isn't distracting anyone, let yourself sleep. You probably need the rest. Many people don't get enough sleep or the quality of their sleep isn't very restful. It's actually possible to sleep and not really rest, as sleep and rest are two different things. Be patient. Your body is re-programming itself. Allow the balancing process to occur without trying to control it or feeling bummed out.

2. Boredom and/or restlessness. Boredom is the result of habitual distraction. The distracted state is the new normal in our culture. We don't even realize we're distracted. When distracted—habitually or not—we're unable to notice the finer details of our experience.

The essential causes of distraction:

*   Not being grounded deep enough in practice and "floating off." When "floating off" occurs, just return your attention to your anchor of focus. If you haven't chosen an anchor, allow yourself to find one. Don't get caught up in decision-making. It's just an anchor. Any anchor will do.

- Entering a plateau where things seem to empty out or go flat (the blahs, basically) either as a momentary experience or as a longer term phase. If you find yourself on a plateau, do one of two things:

    a. If you're focusing on an anchor, you can stay the course and let it be okay that practice isn't exciting. You make just as much progress on "blah" days as on the dramatic ones.

    b. Or, try switching your anchor to something new. If you don't have an anchor, picking one might strengthen your sense of purpose.

3. Seemingly random emotions. Sometimes emotions suddenly emerge, such as anger, joy, or sadness. Maybe you find yourself crying but don't actually feel
   sad. What to do? Realize this is old stuff coming up and working itself out. Most of it isn't possible to figure out, nor is it usually worth the time. By the time you're able to sort it out, the emotion is gone and no longer relevant.

At some point, you'll realize that meditation isn't just one process, but many—or a large, over-arching process made up of infinitely smaller processes leading all the way back to our subconscious.

Here are two amazing occurrences that tend to encourage us:

1. We find that we are suddenly able to maintain focus way longer than normal. Maybe the practice abruptly moves from challenging to super easy. Don't get attached to these positive, desirable feelings.

   Don't spend too much time trying to find out how to have these feelings more often. They might not continue no matter what you do. You can have a seemingly perfect practice one day and a seemingly disastrous one the next.

2. We rest into a deep, quiet place beyond or between thoughts. We're usually unaware that we're in a deep state of meditation until after it's over. It's easy to long to return to these deep states as often as possible. Unfortunately, the return is less likely to happen when we try too hard to get there. So again, best not to put too much value on deep experiences.

Now let's consider how to navigate the ups and downs in the long-term.

First, the downs. Sometimes things seem effortless and smooth. Other times, we're bouncing around in our mind like we're on a wild horse—or even worse, we feel like the horse is dragging us through one rough patch after another.

Do we let go of the reins and cut our losses for the session, or do we hang on and hope the ride gets smoother again?

What happens while practicing matters less than how we react to what's happening. Did you get that? Read it again.

Over time, we realize the power of meditation is that we have a choice about how we react to our experience. We know we can say, "Wow, this is certainly challenging and bothersome" and move on, or we can react more strongly and say, "I HATE this." Maybe we get downright prickly, but we don't have to get prickly about being prickly.

Now for the ups. The opposite is also true and in some ways harder to accept. We choose not to fall in love with desirable experiences and just recognize: "Wow, this is great ... while it lasts, that is." The wisest choice in the long run is not to get attached.

Hating or loving, just watch experience and choose not to react as often as you can. You're looking for the natural meditative place in yourself, not aspiring to be a technical mediation master.

Don't sweat it

Avoid beating yourself up over losing control of your practice. The wild horse has its way now and then. You might not believe it, but wild moments are actually good for you because they rip the control freak right out of you.

Beating yourself up is senseless violence and just another crude form of distraction! You can't beat yourself up and be aware at the same time.

Besides, when you beat yourself up, you sweat. Stay cool. Be a kick-ass meditator instead of kicking your meditator-self.

Too busy to meditate? Of course you are

You are most definitely too busy to meditate. You fill your life to the brim. If there's an empty moment, you find something to fill it with—right? Let's put aside for now the discussion about how healthy this habit is. (You know anyway, don't you?)

A few ways to handle being too busy to practice:

- Set your alarm early, sit up in bed, prop yourself up with pillows, close your eyes.

- At red lights, open eyes, soften gaze, take deep breaths, and turn music off (or on, if that will help).

- Schedule it—like all non-negotiable things you must do.

- In the shower, pause your movement, close your eyes, feel the water, listen to the sound, and notice how you feel physically and otherwise.

- A few minutes before bedtime, get into bed, prop yourself up with pillows, and close your eyes.

Meditating through life's rough patches

Meditators come in two types—those who practice more earnestly during tough times, and those who drop out of practice. No one escapes tough times in life. Some of us are better than others at coping.

Meditation can help, although at the time of trouble it might not seem so. It can actually bring us closer to our sorrow, anxiety, fears, and other feelings we want to wipe away—like that friend who always nudges you to be honest with yourself, much to your chagrin.

We can appreciate being reminded of a truth even when we're not ready to accept that truth.

During difficult times, practice under the umbrella of these truths:

- Meditation isn't a way to check out and avoid suffering. Respect your suffering as the challenging and worthy opponent it is. Oppose, but don't fight or try to escape.

- Your practice might seem negatively impacted by your suffering. Don't judge yourself or try to maintain your former higher level of practice. Doing so will double the suffering—first in life, then in meditation.

- Don't be surprised if you uncover a pearl of wisdom that wouldn't have emerged had you not been suffering.

- Your thoughts have the potential to be your best friend or worst enemy during tough times. Don't chase away bad thoughts or chase after good ones. Stay positive or neutral, but not falsely so. If you feel bad, just feel it. There is insight in everything.

What to do when shifts happen

If you keep a journal, you're especially likely to notice changes. Change has occurred, no doubt. But the real cause for celebration is that alongside a change in habits, an actual shift in consciousness has occurred. This is huge.

Sure, you might not feel that different. You're still you!

Meditation makes us more ourselves. We don't become someone else.

Take some time to really savor the changes you've made. Cultivate a taste for watching your shifts as they occur. This is a mindfulness practice in and of itself.

Here are a few little green sprouts to keep an eye out for as they pop from the fertile field of your first phase of practice:

- Others notice you that you look really well, seem at ease, or are more alert. Other people often see us more clearly than we see ourselves.

- You notice more about others and the world around you. You're more relaxed, open, and aware. You really are seeing more clearly.

- You catch yourself before you react to situations, especially those you have less control over, recognizing that you have a choice.

- You notice more things about yourself that you like and want to nurture, as well as those you'd like to change.

- You notice bodily sensation and experience more often and on a more subtle level, beyond basic levels of pain and pleasure.

- You notice things in your practice you would never have noticed in earlier phases, such as when to tweak your sitting posture to refresh your attention.

- You instinctively know how to adjust your concentration, widen or narrow awareness, or shift focus entirely.

In the section called "The inner toolbox," we explored how these shifts occur on a more technical level and the vital role we play in shaping them.

To make the best use of these tools, seek out a good teacher to share reflections with, check in with, and guide you further along as your journey becomes more nuanced.

Even if you can't afford to pay for guidance, seek a good free resource online, for example. You might even find someone willing to work in person for free. Newer meditation guides will often offer guidance for free, not only to learn, but also to make contacts and build good karma. For these same reasons, even some master teachers offer free guidance from time to time.

Meditation is more than a quiet place

We're drawn to the quiet, empty spaces in consciousness. But if quiet was all we were seeking, we'd spend more time in the library. In addition to quieting our minds, meditation increases our intuition, warms our hearts, and sharpens our skills. We get a taste of how powerful we actually are. The so-called quiet mind is actually a mighty dynamo.

We also see with ever-increasing clarity our patterns of thought, sensations, and feelings. Even our patterns of breath become clearer. We see the patterns we want to nurture and refine, as well as those that aren't productive and can be let go.

We notice when we're reacting or are about to react. We catch ourselves before losing control of the train. We also see a true, ever-changing reality of our world and ourselves. We are set free, understanding that there's nothing to hold on to, but much to flow along with.

The mind in meditation has been compared to the uninterrupted flow of oil from one vessel to another—just a steady stream of smooth, rich presence, filling up while also emptying out. There is no beginning, no end.

Many moments, many approaches

Classical philosophy has spoken of absolute truth as a pathless land, as well as a land made of many paths. A pathless land is more like an open field where there are no paths and every blade of grass is pristine, similar to the state of Nirvana. When resting in Nirvana, one is also resting in absolute truth. There are no choices to make. Even consciousness is "choiceless."

The seeker can enter the field from any direction, walk in any direction, turn corners, make U-turns, go in circles, jump up and down, depart the field, re-enter from another place, stand still, do a happy dance, and start another round in infinite variations. Still the grass is pristine and untouched.

No particular path ever gets worn because every inch of the field is a path.

However, the seeker is free to visualize a path and even to follow it as the "right" way. Doing so requires her to necessarily block out the rest of the field. In doing this, she hasn't discovered a truth—she has chosen one.

Choosing favorites is fine, but any favorite will let you down at some point. As many moments as we have to practice are as many moments as we have choices to make.

Some of us choose an approach and stick with it for life, deepening our insight into its unique view of Meditative Truth. Others choose different approaches on different days, or even switch approaches during a single session without a reason. Maybe the approach being explored at a particular moment isn't even a learned one, but one the practitioner is "discovering" in real-time.

Having too few or too many choices can be a curse or a blessing, depending on where we are in our journey and how we react to our circumstances. Do we give up, wander aimlessly, repeat the same practice with indifference, indulge ourselves, get lost, throw a hissy fit, or find insight? There are so many ways to react.

One thing is certain. What we do depends largely on how much we value our deeper self and the way we show up in life.

Choose the practice that's right for you and explore it as your core practice so long as it serves you. When a core practice no longer serves you, explore another. If you don't know which practice is right for you, keep searching—on the same path, through many paths, or "pathlessly."

You're worth it.

Your map is the way; your tools are the means. Trust that you're as ready as possible and when/if all else fails, remember that you're not alone. You have your meditation friends, teachers, this companion book, and thousands of years of wisdom from those who traveled the road before you. Remember: Even the road least travelled is a well-worn path.

Thanks

To Patrick Ryan, my partner in this life, for doing whatever it took on any given day to help me get through the writing and release of this book.

To ShiwaniSrivastava, for her insight, economy with words, for helping me clarify what needed to be saidand for being so genuine, sunny and easygoing.

And to everyone else who has helped make this possible with advice, critique, and guidance.

To those who show up to my workshops, corporate programs, retreats, private studio, and classes.

Andespecially, to you, the reader.

Thank you,

Tina Foster
San Francisco, California
October, 2014

www.fosterandflourish.com
www.meditationfornonmeditators.com

Twitter:(@fosterandflo) and/or (@4everbeginners)

My Facebook page: www.facebook.com/FosterandFlourish

Actually, we're just beginning…

I hope you've enjoyed this as much as I have. In some ways, I wish I could stay on the train with you forever, but I'd just keep talking about meditation and you'd never get a chance to practice.

I believe the journey of meditation is so vital to us as individuals, as well as in relationship to one another, the world, and future worlds. I believe that meditation is just as natural as sleeping and eating, and also as powerful.

Once meditation settles back into everyday life, it doesn't require any more effort than taking a nap or having a snack.

I hope this book helps you wake up to and fall in love with your meditative self and your meditation practice. I hope your practice becomes your companion. I promise you it will never let you down.

Likewise, I hope you return to this book many times and stay tuned for future editions that will surely come your way. I intend to keep it as current and relevant as possible and to add to it as needed. You can be a big part of this by letting me know what you think.

Feel free to contact me anytime via email:
Tina@MeditationForNonMeditators.com

Most important…

A new tool that helps us live better is like a new toy in some ways. We get excited and are turned on by the novelty, until the magic eventually wears off. That's okay. Yourbreak from practice is like hitting the pause button. Let's set an intention together to your long-term shift and never-ending growth…

You might fall in and out of practice countless times. Meditation practice is just like that friend you don't see for ages, but whom you can talk to like you just saw them yesterday.

I look forward to future journeys with you.

If you'd like to be among the first to know when the next book in the series is coming out, and perhaps be a little closer to the creative process, sign up for my main mailing list here: http://www.fosterandflourish.com

And if this book has helped you, there are two things that I'd love you to help with:

1. Recommend this book to anyone and everyone you think it could benefit. They'll be more likely to read a book you recommend to them than one recommended by experts. That's a proven fact of marketing.

2. The second is to review (in earnest) this book on Amazon. Reviews help in several ways, including making books easier to find in searches.

Thank you in advance, from the bottom of my heart, for reviewing.

About Other Books in the Meditation for Non-Meditators Series

- *Meditation for Non-Meditators: A (Forever) Beginner's Guide* (released July 2013) - A fun, light introduction to meditation featuring three Guided Practices. 17 pages, illustrated

- *More Meditation for Non-Meditators: Guided Practices for Everyone (coming in 2015)*

Use these books as:

- Essential resources for solo practitioners, as well as for teachers, coaches, therapists, or anyone who guides others in meditation
- A simple, fun, modern, but well-seasoned approach to meditation
- Illustrated guides. Each book is beautifully designed to help guide you into the meditative place in yourself.

PRAISE FOR THIS BOOK SERIES:

"Holy sh*t balls, you've nailed it...for the first time in my life, I do not feel guilty for not being able to meditate and calm my mind! This is BRILLIANT!!!"—Kat Mikic, online marketing strategist

"These guided meditations are accessible, easy to understand, and light and airy in instruction. [They] won't leave a newbie feeling overwhelmed. The language cuts through strict tradition, dogma, religious structure, and any new age woo-woo."—Shauna Brandes, birth doula & restorative yoga instructor

"Tina writes with such great acceptance for the natural obstacles that come with the terrain of working with the mind. I'm particularly struck by her unique and creative naming of the experience."—Ralph de la Rosa, founder of The Mindfulness Sessions

More about Tina Foster

Tina was born in the mid-sixties in Huntsville, Alabama, a high-tech town known as "The Rocket City" that sprawls around the caves, marshes, and springs of the Appalachian foothills.

She has also lived in Athens, Georgia; Brno, Czech Republic; New Orleans, Louisiana. She currently lives in the Mission District of San Francisco.

Here are some other random facts about Tina:

- She got her B.A. Degree in English Language and Literature and Media Arts.
- She began practicing Hatha yoga in the late '80s, but was unable to sit in meditation until decades later.
- For the astrologically interested, Tina is: Double Aries, Pisces Moon, pretty much everything else in Virgo. Wood Snake in the Chinese system. She's a yogi of 3+ decades, yet has no idea why she's never had her Vedic chart done.
- Jungian archetype: Alchemist; Secondary: Creator
- Spirit Animal: Hummingbird
- Favorite food and drink: Anything from the coconut
- Favorite thing to do for fun: Walking in cities, hiking in wilderness